How to Analyze People

21 Fundamental Techniques to Interpret Body Language, Personality Types, Human Psychology, and Secretly Analyze People

David T Abbots

Your Free Gift

As a way of saying thank you for your purchase, I wanted to offer you a free bonus E-book called **5 Incredible Hypnotic Words To Influence Anyone**

Download the free guide here: https://www.subscribepage.com/b1b5i8

If your trying to persuade or influence other people then words are the most important tool you have to master.

As Humans we interact with words, we shape the way we think through words, we express ourselves through words. Words evoke feelings and have the ability to talk to the lister's subconscious.

In this free guide, you'll discover 5 insanely effective words that you can easily use to start hypnotizing anyone in conversation.

Listen to this book for free

Do you want to be able to listen to this book whenever you want? Maybe whilst driving to work or running errands. It can be difficult nowadays to sit down and listen to a book. So I am really excited to let you know that this book is available in audio format. What's great is you can get this book for FREE as part of a 30-day audible trial. Thereafter if you don't want to stay an Audible member you can cancel, but keep the book.

Benefits of signing up to audible:
- After the trial, you get 1 free audiobook and 2 free audio originals each month
- Can roll over any unused credits
- Choose from over 425,000 + titles
- Listen anywhere with the Audible app and across multiple devices
- Keep your audiobooks forever, even if you cancel your membership

Click below to get started
Audible US - https://tinyurl.com/yxp99y2n
Audible UK - https://tinyurl.com/y6q5cadt
Audible FR - https://tinyurl.com/y2ksqbqk
Audible DE - https://tinyurl.com/yxqnqbsj

Table of Contents

Introduction

"You don't need to be a top-notch interrogator to figure out what is going on in someone's head. The signals are always there--all you need to do is know what to look for."- LaRae

You really don't have to be an FBI investigator to read people or know what exactly they are thinking. A person is almost always giving away his personality, attitude, beliefs, ideologies, likes, dislikes, values and more through signals, if you are perceptive enough to catch those signals. I just read an article today about how what you "like" on Facebook can help the social media giant decipher everything from your gender to your sexuality to your relationship status. There are clues everywhere about people, pretty much offered by them consciously or unconsciously.

You don't realize that people are giving away these clues or signals about them because you are not watching out for it. Once you know exactly what to look for while reading people, you'll be more perceptive towards these signals. Trust me; it is as exciting as solving a challenging puzzle. People can be enigmatic and mysterious. However, a smart people watcher can quickly decipher an individual's personality through their verbal and nonverbal clues.

The ability to analyze people drastically impacts the manner in which you deal with them. When you understand how the other person feels and thinks, you can tailor your message in a way that is best understood by the other person.

Did you know research conducted by MIT concluded that body language alone could determine the outcome of negotiations accurately 80 percent of the time? This simply means people are giving away clues about their innermost thoughts and feelings (probably, things in their subconscious which they aren't even aware of) all the time.

Many things account for an individual's behavior, personality, beliefs, values, and attitude, fundamentally childhood experiences, birth order (yes even the order in which we are born impacts our personality), gender roles, genes, peer behavior and more. Indicators of all these factors are evident in the manner in which a person speaks or conducts himself.

While a layman will look at people scratching their nose as a harmless gesture (it can be harmless of course within the context of say a fly sat on his nose), a people analyzer always looks for a deeper meaning within the context. For instance, if a person has been confronted with something and begins scratching his nose, he is more often than not lying. These are simple and seemingly harmless gestures that reveal a lot about an individual.

The key to understanding and profiling people around you is to pause and closely observe them. It is to see beyond what they show, to hear beyond what they speak.

Every person is like an onion. They have different layers of personality that you need to mentally peel to decode their real traits and persona. Some layers are visible to others, while the innermost layers are something known (or at times unknown, even to them) only to them.

There are many things that you need to pay close attention to if you want to read people with the finesse of a professional psycho analyzer. It can be anything from what a particular person does in his or her spare time to his or her hobbies. For instance, if you get to know that a person attends church during his or spare time, you quickly conclude that he or she is religious. If they are regularly contributing to community activities or volunteering during their spare time, they may be philanthropic, empathetic or socially conscious by nature.

Someone who parties may have an endless zest for the good things in life, while someone who spends hours in front of the television may be low on drive. See, even something as seemingly inconsequential as what a person does in his or her free time indicates their personality.

Some psychologists are of the opinion that a person often gravitates towards things he thinks he lacks to compensate for the same. So, you may look for more friends and social approval because you don't believe you are good enough.

Notice how people are keenly interested in zodiac and sun signs? Isn't that an indication of low self-understanding? People are mainly interested in pursuing things to compensate for what they lack or things that take them in the direction of a clear goal. When people don't get attention, they become showy. People who present a tough exterior may do it to hide their painful past of being bullied as children.

There are subtle clues everywhere. You just need to be alert and watch out for them. I'd suggest starting with yourself. Test your knowledge by analyzing your personality. Next, move towards analyzing the personality of people who are close to you. Eventually, move to strangers at supermarket, airports, coffee shops, etc. to sharpen your people insights. It won't happen overnight.

However, with consistent practice, you will be able to quickly tell about a person simply by looking at them or interacting with them for a while. This will help you communicate in a more mutually beneficial manner with the individual. Think about a scenario, where you are going to negotiate a deal. If you identify what the person is thinking or feeling about the deal, you can modify your speech and body language to tackle their reservations or doubts about the deal, thus winning it in your favor in the end.

This is what sales professionals, orators, leaders and other influencers do all the time. They understand who they are selling or talking to and then tailor their message to inspire the person's trust.

I know car sales professionals who are trained to look at what's inside your car for clues about your likes. For instance, if they find a golf kit in the back, they'll start a conversation about how they are looking to enjoy a good game of golf this weekend. The passionate golf player is elated that the salesperson is as interested in golf as he or she is- their amazing ice-breaker! What did the salesperson do? He simply observed and got you talking about what you love to build rapport, and eventually get you to buy from him.

Every person has a unique personality that impacts the way we relate to him or her. Does a person exhibit a predominantly introvert or extrovert personality? Is he or she primarily driven by relationships or material goals? How does the person handle uncertainty? What is it that feeds the person's ego? How is the person's behavior when he or she is stressed or frustrated? How does the person behave when he or she is relaxed?

Introduction

Are you ready to read 21 power-packed tips about analyzing a person using a series of fascinating and proven techniques?

Chapter One:
What People's Body Language
Reveals about Them

Body language is an inexhaustible source of information about a person's mind. It offers an astounding amount of information about a person's thoughts, feelings, and beliefs. Reading people becomes easier when you know what to look for. We are invariably wired to pick up body language clues even when we aren't consciously aware of it. According to a UCLA research, 7 percent of all communication relies on words, 38 percent comes from our voice, and a staggering 55 percent comes from body language.

Here are some of the most reliable and proven clues for developing greater insights into a person's thoughts and feelings.

1. Body Language

Crossed Legs and Arms

Crossed legs and arms are subconscious physical barriers that reveal that the other person is not open to listening to what you are saying or doesn't believe you. Even if they have a friendly smile plastered on their face or speaking in a courteous manner, their gestures tell a different story. Psychologically, crossing arms and feet is a signal of physically and emotionally shutting yourself from what is before you. The fact that it is subconscious and involuntary makes it near accurate.

Genuine Smiles

How do you tell a fake smile from a genuine one? Mouths often lie, but our eyes reveal the truth. A genuine smile often reaches the eyes and crinkles the skin around the eyes to form crow's feet. Many people offer fake smiles to conceal what they are truly feeling. However, look for crinkles near the eyes the next time you want to figure out if the smile is indeed real.

Postures Tell Stories Too

When several people walk into a room, how do you identify the leader or influencer of the group? The effect is mostly determined by the way they walk and their posture. They will more often than not have an erect posture or walk straight, with their shoulders pulled back in an authoritative position. They subconsciously try to occupy as much space as possible or try to fill as much space as possible with their presence to signify power.

Pulling your shoulders behind expands your frame and makes your frame appear bigger. Similarly, slouching is reducing your form and occupies lesser space to reveal powerlessness.

People who shuffle their posture or position often lack self-confidence or direction. This is also true for individuals whose head faces downwards most of the time. If you notice someone with these body language signals, they may need extra motivation and encouragement to boost their confidence. They may be inhibited or unsure of their ideas, and asking them direct questions can help draw these ideas or suggestions out of them.

It's all in the Eyes

Do you recall the time when your parents and teachers scolded you and asked you to look into their eyes while talking? The primary idea was that it is challenging to hold another person's gaze when you are not speaking the truth. They weren't too off the mark. However, now this knowledge has become so widely shared that liars intentionally hold their gaze for longer than required, which should give you a good idea of their integrity. If you are speaking to someone whose unblinking stare is making you uncomfortable, they may be trying to hide something or lying to you.

Excessive Nodding

When you are speaking to someone or group of people, the ones nodding their head in an exaggerated manner are the ones who are most worried about approval. They are deeply concerned about the impression you have of them and, and are eager to gain your approval.

Stress Signals

Clenched jaws, furrowed brows, and stiff necks are often a sign of stress and anxiety.

Chapter One: What People's Body Language Reveals about Them

Irrespective of what the person may be speaking, he or she is under some form of internal discomfort. They may be uncomfortable about the topic of discussion, or they are thinking about a pressing problem that is causing them stress. The idea is to look out for a clear discrepancy between what the person is saying and their body language.

Nervousness and Anxiety

Excessive blinking and facial movements are a sign of nervousness. Similarly, people who are nervous tend to fidget with their hands and don't let them stay in a single place. Tapping fingers and feet are also a sign of nervousness. Notice how people who are nervous almost unconsciously develop jittery feet.

Feet Direction

When people speak or communicate, the direction of their feet is the last thing on their mind, which makes this unconscious act fairly reliable. The direction in which a person's feet point indicates where they are heading during a conversation. So if a person's feet point towards the door even if they are turning and looking in your direction, they want to escape as soon as possible. Notice how when you are engaged in an enjoyable conversation with someone, your foot instinctively steps forward!

Attraction Body Language

I can write an entire book on this one, but it's sufficient to say that there are typical signs that a person is drawn to you. Of course, there are several factors due to which the language of attraction can vary from person to person. However, in general, leaning in the direction of the person you are speaking to or tilting your head reveal that you are interested in the person or conversation.

Another huge subconscious sign that a person is attracted to you is when he or she starts mirroring your actions. Self-grooming gestures such as running their hands through their hair or straitening their tie/scarf or standing too close to you (we'll look at proxemics later) are signs of attraction. However, expression of attraction also largely depends on an individual's personality type. An introvert may express his or her attraction in a manner that is different from an extrovert.

Shaking Hands

A firm handshake or strong grip is more or less a sign of trust and power. The person is looking forward to a positive long-term association. It is a signal that he or she is mentally present and focused on you and will most likely give his or her all to the partnership or association in future. A limp handshake reveals a weak and potentially dishonest persona.

Similarly, when a person shakes his hand with his or palms facing downwards, he or she is trying to reveal their power or authority over you. They are keen to dominate the association and have their way as much as possible.

2. Walk

People who have a heavy gait combined with a low gravity center may signify some sort of pain, frustration or depression. People who are extremely driven and confident, walk fast and in a single direction. Their posture is more upright.

On the other hand, people who walk at a slower pace are more reflective, and there's an internal dialogue going on within them almost all the time. People who are more driven by emotions tend to change their pace or direction often during the course of walking. When people feel vulnerable, they walk with their arms crossed just above the waist.

A person taking more slow and timid steps may be an indication of low confidence or self-esteem. He or she may need more encouragement to be sure of himself or herself. It reflects how people approach life.

You can also predict the dynamics of a relationship simply by observing a couple walking together. If one person walks ahead of the other, he or she is either dominating the relationship or playing the role of a protector within the relationship. They may also want to lead, grab all the limelight and be the more aggressive partner in the relationship. Although, again this can change according to culture (more on cultural context later).

3. Tone

The tone of an individual's voice can reveal plenty about how he or she is feeling. If the person is not speaking in an even tone or there are plenty of inconsistencies in the tone throughout his or her speech, they are more likely angry, nervous or excited. It can also be a signal of concealing important information.

Similarly, look out for the volume in which the individual is speaking. When people speak in a volume that is softer than their regular voice, something may not be right.

The tone with which a person speaks can give a lot of meaning to the communication irrespective of what he or she is saying. For instance, notice how people say something seemingly nice on your face but their sarcastic or acidic tone is a total giveaway of what they really think about you. These are people who possess a passive-aggressive personality, who want to hit back albeit in a non-obvious, unaggressive manner. The same words can carry entirely different connotations when they are spoken with a different tone and voice inflection.

For example, the manner in which you finish a sentence or the words you emphasize on can mean different things even if you are using the same words. If people finish a sentence on a high note, they are most likely asking a question or inquiring with a sense of uncertainty or suspicious. Similarly, when someone finishes their sentence in a more flat or even note, it means they are making a statement and not raising doubts. This makes the person come across as more authoritative and assured.

Also, take a sentence like, "Did you steal the ring?" It can have different connotations when the person emphasizes on different words. If the emphasis is on the word "you" they are trying to ascertain whether you stole it or someone else did it. On the other hand, if they emphasize on "ring," they are ascertaining whether you stole the ring or something else.

4. Tips for Reading Body Accurately

Establish a Baseline for Analyzing People

It is vital to have a clear frame or baseline for observing a person's behavior. Of course, this is not always possible, especially when you are meeting new people. However, having a baseline for studying someone's behavior offers you greater insights about them. It gives you a more comprehensive and in-depth overview of his or her personality.

For instance, imagine a person you know closely is a hyperactive, fast-thinking individual who is always charged up about doing things. He or she just can't sit still and is always brimming with ideas. Now, a person who doesn't know this bundle of energy will quickly conclude through his body language that he or she is nervous. The fidgety signals, tapping hands, bouncing feet are all typical signs of nervousness. People who haven't established a baseline for the person's basic disposition will be led to believe that he or she is nervous and not hyper-energetic or excited about doing things all the time.

You need to gain more information or understanding of a person's fundamental nature to read their body language more accurately. How do they typically behave or react in different situations and settings? How they speak and express their ideas and emotions? What is the typical tone of their voice when they experience different emotions? Does it transform when they are excited, sad or nervous? How do they communicate their interest and disinterest about a thing? These are all important insights that will help you read the person more effectively. It will reduce potential inaccuracies in analyzing the person.

When there is a clear mismatch in their baseline behavior, you can tell something is not right. You can keep a close eye on nonverbal expression patterns that are not consistent with their normal behavior.

Look For Clue Clusters

The biggest fallacy people tend to make when it comes to studying people through their body language is that they look for isolated clues rather than analyzing a series of clues together. For example, if you read that maintaining eye contact is a signal of confidence and honesty, you'll conclude only on the basis on a person's consistent eye contact that he or she is a confident and truthful individual.

All other signs that point to the opposite direction such as sweating, twitching toes and touching the face frequently (signs of nervousness or dishonesty) will be ignored because you've made a sweeping conclusion based on a single clue. To arrive at a reasonably accurate conclusion about a person's behavior, you have to look out for a group of clues across posture, gestures, expressions and voice tone. It is easy to fake one clue (for instance maintaining eye contact) to mislead the reader. However, it is near impossible to manipulate a cluster of clues that point to a specific direction.

Context and Setting

Don't jump to a conclusion about people without understanding the context or setting. For instance, a person may be stiff and formal when you meet them at their workplace, and the same person may be extremely gregarious and effervescent when you meet them at an office party at the bar. The setting plays a vital role in reading people. You may conclude that the person who is simply relaxed is casual about his or her work and doesn't take co-workers seriously. It is nothing but the setting that allows him or her to relax and open up.

Similarly, context is also important. A person may sit crossing his or her arms and legs not because he or she is closed to the idea of listening to you but simply because of its freezing cold.

Likewise, a person may be leaning in the opposite direction because they may be uncomfortable with the seating. Sometimes rubbing your nose constantly can simply mean you have a cold. This is why when you depend on nonverbal clues for analyzing a person; identify a minimum of 2-3 signals that point to the conclusion. Also, rely on different nonverbal communication avenues than a single one. Consider a person's voice tone, walk, posture, hand gestures, facial expressions, feet movements, etc. collectively. This will increase your chances of reading a person near accurately.

Consider the setting. For instance, if a person is being interviewed for a job, he or she may simply be nervous, which is why they may not maintain eye contact or run their hand over their face multiple times. This doesn't necessarily mean they are lying.

Cultural Context

Though smiling, maintaining eye contact and other body language expressions are universal, some gestures and expressions can have different connotations and a different culture, which means we may misread other cultures through our own cultural filters. Have a baseline or cultural context for studying people belonging to other cultures.

For instance, people in the Italian culture are known to be extremely vivacious and loud in their expressions. They gesticulate in an excited and loud manner with a high pitched voice, marked by plenty of shouting. This is their way of communicating affection and enthusiasm.

Someone who comes from a culture where enthusiasm is not openly expressed (think England), may not interpret this non-verbal behavior accurately. Viewing things in a cultural framework or backdrop makes it easier to deal with people across cultures. Similarly, a single gesture can have different interpretations throughout cultures. For example, the thumbs-up sign is a gesture signifying validation or luck in western cultures. However, in some parts of Middle East, it is not considered culturally appropriate to flash the thumbs-up gesture.

Even when it comes to personal space, people from western countries often strive to keep some space or a physical barrier (such as a handbag, etc.) while interacting with strangers or when they meet people for the first time. It signifies that they want their personal space to be respected. Not noting these differences may cost you your international business deals.

Chapter Two:
Eye Movements and Facial Expressions

5. Eye Movements

Your eye movements are closely linked with specific areas of the brain to cause certain movements as your brain functions. If I ask to recall the sound of the person you idolized as a child, your eyes will most likely move a little up and then to the left as you visualize your childhood hero.

Then they'll move a little downwards and to the right when you start imagining the voice of your idol. Nope, I am not spying on you. There is a pattern to your eye movements based on which section of the brain is processing information or function at that time. Your brain nerves are connected with the eyes to cause very specific movements when a certain section of the brain is working. Hence, paying close attention to a person's eye movements can reveal a lot about his or her persona.

Visual Memory

When you ask a person about information that isn't easily available in the memory, the eyes will most likely move to the upper left. It means they are trying to recall past information. This is common among people who are more visual learners and depend on their visual memory for pulling out information. When a person moves his or eyes to upper right when confronted with a question, they are more often than not speaking the truth and simply trying to recall information from memory to give you an answer.

When you ask a person where they had been yesterday, and they look to the left instead of right (trying to recall), they are most likely not speaking the truth. Instead of recalling information, they are trying to construct their own version of where they were.

Internal Dialogue

When a person is grabbling with an internal debate or dilemma, they will mostly glance in the direction of the left collarbone. This simply indicates that a person is deeply thinking about something, engaged in an internal conflict or questioning something through an inner

dialogue. This is the most likely eye movement
when you confront a person, and he or she is
torn between telling the truth and lying.

Eyes moving laterally from one side to another
quickly can be an indication of lying or looking
for some form of escape on being caught. It can
also happen when people are creating
conspiracies in their mind when they think no
one is watching or listening.

Recalling Sound

When a person is trying to recall a particular
sound, their eyes move in the right lateral
direction. This is a neat trick to assess if people
are really reciting lines in the mind when they
claim to. Notice how small children will have
their eyes in the right lateral when they repeat
lines/sounds they've heard from their parents or
elders.

Similarly, when someone is making up (or lying)
about a conversation they supposedly had, their
eyes will move in the left lateral direction. It
demonstrates the fact that they are creating a
sound that doesn't exist in the first place.

Kinesthetic or Feelings

When a person remembers the feeling or sensation or a specific thing, his or her eyes move to the lower right side. You can try this for yourself. Try to imagine the sensation of satin on your body by closing your eyes. You will gradually notice your eyes moving in the lower right direction involuntarily.

Attraction

When a person is attracted to you or is deeply interested in what you are saying, their pupil size will expand. Similarly, when the subject is changed to something that is boring or doesn't hold their attention, the size will contract almost immediately.

Similarly, if a person is blinking more than normal while interacting with you (over 6-10 times a minute), they are most likely attracted to you. The feelings he or she processes in his or her mind towards you subconsciously impacts your blink rate. This is exactly why blinking is closely associated with flirting.

When someone likes you, his or her eyes will shine in your presence. It isn't all romantic;

there's boring physiology behind it. When we are attracted to someone, our eyes become slightly moist, which in turn allows them to reflect greater light. Thus, on spotting shiny eyes, you should dig deeper and look at other clues indicating attraction.

Looking Upwards and Downwards

Looking upwards and downwards presents seizing up a person or evaluating them either as a threat or a potential sexual mate. It is often offensive to the person who is being seized as comes across as gaining dominance over the person or looking down upon them. It is almost like the person is saying, "you are not as powerful as me, and hence you will surrender to the gaze."

Potential Errors

Again, unlike most people analyzing techniques, this one isn't foolproof. External stimuli such as sound and light can influence eye movements. The pressure to consistently keep eye contact can also lead to inaccuracies in reading people. If you don't discover a clear movement of eyes, watch out for excessive flickering in a single direction.

Also, the way people process information in the minds differs from person to person based on the sense that is most dominant in them. While some people process information visually, others are auditory creatures.

If you ask someone to describe events as they saw it, they may access their visual memory by moving the eyes to the upper left, but if they are fundamentally auditory creatures, they will also form auditory information of the event by moving their eyes in the right lateral direction.

You've got to identify the sense that rules a person before attempting to read their eye movements. How do you do that? Focus on the words they use while expressing their thoughts, feelings, and emotions. Do they frequently use words such as, "I see your point of view, or I see where you are coming from," they are mostly visual creatures? Similarly, when they emphasize on words such as "I hear that" or "I hear you," they are more often than not dominated by the auditory sense.

You also have to determine whether a person is right or left handed because then the two are ruled by different sides of the brain. So if a person is ruled by the right side of his brain and is left-handed, the reverse may be true for them. This means, when they recall information, their eyes may move to the right, and when they are making up information, their eyes may move to the left.

6. Facial Expressions

Examine Full Face

Facial expressions comprise multiple regions of the face. For instance, if a person is surprised, typically his or her eyebrows will be pulled up, the upper eyelids will widen, and the mouth will drop open. Again, one of the biggest mistakes people make while reading facial expressions is looking for single expressions in one region of the face without considering the entire face.

For example, raising eyebrows can be a signal of both fear and amazement. If you want to know which of these emotions is causing the person to raise his or her eyebrows, you have to watch out for other facial clues. Sometimes, people also raise their eyebrows while emphasizing certain parts of their speech.

When the expressions associated with one emotion is a subset of emotions associated with another (amazement or surprise is often a subset of the expressions associated with fear), you have to watch out for other clues.

In this example, if a person is scared, their eyebrows will be pulled up (together), with the lower eyelid being more tensed and the corner of their lips will be pulled back. On the other hand, if the person is surprised, their eyebrows will most likely be pulled up, and their jaw will be slightly lowered. Thus looking at the entire face can give you a more comprehensive reading of what the person is feeling.

Micro Expressions

Microexpressions occur in a matter of split seconds, which makes it near impossible to fake. For example, when a person is resorting to deception, his or her mouth will slant a little. Similarly, immediately after they have uttered the lie, their eyes will roll for a fraction of a second. These micro-expressions are so involuntary and subconscious that they cannot be manipulated or contrived unlike say maintaining constant eye contact.

When a person is lying, the color of his or her cheeks may change slightly and quickly. Similarly, their nostrils may flare and/, or they may bite their lips (a subconscious gesture revealing that they are preventing themselves from blurting out the truth). The eye movements also become quicker. These signals point to the direction that the person is processing false information.

Focus on Fundamental Emotions

A lot of body language newbies make the mistake of associating an increasingly specific interpretation with a facial expression. That's not how expressions work. There may be several thousands of distinct facial expressions, but they don't necessarily convey a specific meaning similar to words. Instead of assigning overtly narrowed down meanings to expressions, watch out for the primary emotion behind these expressions.

For example, if you are asking who ate the chocolates from the fridge last night, don't look for signals like "ABC" expression means he or she hasn't eaten chocolates; while "XYZ" expressions mean he or she has eaten it.

Rather, focus on the seven fundamental emotions, which have been scientifically proven to be linked with facial expressions. The seven basic emotions are fear, surprise, contempt, disgust, happiness, anger, and sadness. If you want to read a person's facial expressions more effectively, concentrate on identifying basic emotions.

Look At Mixed Emotions

We often experience a series of complex emotions and not an isolated emotion. It isn't rare for people to experience a mix of emotions such as anger, frustration, and sadness. Emotional blend facial expressions often combine movements across emotions. This means different facial expressions can reveal different emotions.

Lips

Lip muscles are delicate and keep shifting to reveal a variety of moods, feelings, and reactions. For instance, pursed lips are an indication of stress, frustration, disproval, and tension. They are trying hard to restrain the expression of their emotions by tightening their lips. It is like holding back words by sealing lips. Puckering is a sign of desire or seduction. It can also be a sign of uncertainty. Pay keen attention to slightly twitching lips. It can be a signal of cynicism, doubt or disbelief in the situation. A person who is lying can give himself or herself away with a split second twitch of the lips.

Have you noticed how sometimes the corner of a person's lips will rise to a single side of their face (referred to as sneering)? It signifies contempt or looking down upon someone's actions. It's almost as if the person is deriving some wicked pleasure while disapproving your acts.

Nose

While the nose may not be as impactful as the mouth or eyes when it comes to reading a person, its prominent location makes it easy to read. Flared nostrils are an indication of displeasure or rage. An unpleasant thought or visual may also cause a person's nose to slightly wrinkle. It also reveals disproval or looking down upon something.

At times, the nose's blood vessels dilate, thus making it appear redder and bigger, which happens when a person is lying. Your parents weren't too off the mark when they told you about how your nose will grow big when you lie. Scratching nose frequently is also a sign of lying.

Eyebrows

Despite the fact that our eyebrows have few muscles linked to them, eyebrows are one of the most conspicuous and suggestive features demonstrating our emotional state. If the forehead is slightly wrinkled and the person's eyebrows are raised, he or she is surprised or questioning your actions. When the eyebrows are slightly lowered, and the eyes are hidden along with a bowed head, it is an indication of hiding emotions.

Eyebrows that slant inwards while being stretched downwards reveal rage or frustration. It can also be a sign of a deep focus on concentration. If there's a horseshoe-like fold between a person's brows, it can be a signal of sadness or disappointment.

Chapter Three:
Reading People through Their Handwriting

Every individual's handwriting is believed to be as distinct as their persona. People's handwriting can offer in-depth insights of their personality. It's not just what a person writes that reveals a lot about who he or she is but also how they write it. Graphology or the study of analyzing people through their handwriting is a good way to go beyond characters written on paper into the person's mind to understand who they really are! Here are a few tips for reading a person through their handwriting.

7. Size of Letters

This is a fundamental observation that can be made while analyzing a person's handwriting. Large letters are an indication of a personality that is gregarious, outgoing, extrovert and sociable. It can also indicate a false sense of pride, confidence or self-importance. There is a sense of showing something that they are not.

Small letters, on the other hand, can represent a shy, unsure and timid personality. It can also be an indication of intense concentration and meticulousness. Midsized letters imply the person is self—assured, flexible and well adjusted.

Gap between Texts

People who write without leaving many gaps between words and letters indicate his or her fear of being alone. These folks love to have lots of people around them and may even find it challenging to respect other people's personal space. People who space out their words/letters are fiercely independent. They place a huge premium on their freedom and do not fancy being overwhelmed by other people's values and opinions.

Letter Shape

Observe the shape of a person's letter to deconstruct their personality. People who write in a more rounded and loopy manner tend to be high on imagination, innovation, artistic prowess, and creativity. Straight, pointed letters indicate an aggressive personality and high intelligence. The person is deep thinking and rational. If the letters are strung together, the individual may be orderly organized and methodical.

Analyzing Individual Letters

The way people construct individual letters reveals a lot about their subconscious thoughts and personality. There are multiple ways of writing a single letter of the alphabet, and each person has their own unique way of writing these letters, which offer wonderful insights into their persona.

For instance, dotting the lower case "i" extremely high is a sign of a free-spirited, independent thinking and creative individual. These individuals tend to be more organized and particular about details. If the dot is in the form of a circle, there are high chances that the person is more childlike and thinks out of the box. Observe closely how people construct their uppercase "I" to know their view about themselves. Is it the same size as the rest of the letters, bigger or smaller? A person who writes a huge uppercase "I" is more often than not overconfident, egoistic and cocky. If the "I" is about the same size as the other letters or smaller, they may be self-assured and happy being who they are.

Notice how people construct their lower case "t" to gather clues into their personality. If they cross the "t" with a fairly long line, it can reveal determination, passion, and enthusiasm. On the other hand, a terse cross across "t" may indicate apathy, lack of interest and low determination. People who cross their "t" high possess a high sense of self-worth and have fairly ambitious goals, while folks who cross their "t" low may be suffering from low self-esteem and may lack ambition.

If the loop in lower case "e" is narrower, the individual is likely to be suspicious or doubtful towards other people. There is some skepticism in them that prevents them from trusting people. These folks tend to be more guarded, reticent and stoic. A wide loop reveals that the individual is more accepting of different people, perspectives, and experiences. They are open to exposing themselves to new ideas and beliefs.

Next, if a person constructs their "o" to reveal a wide, open circle, they are more often than not open individuals who are expressive and don't hesitate to share their secrets about their life. On the other hand, a more closed "o" can be a sign of someone who fiercely guards their privacy and is more reserved by nature.

Cursive Letters

Cursive writing can offer clues that printed or regular writing may sometimes miss, which means if you want a more comprehensive reading you should consider both.

Consider how people write the lower case "I" to know more about the person. If there's a narrower loop in the letter, it can be a signal of stress owing to limiting oneself. Similarly, a wide loop indicates that the person is not very structured or doesn't go by a set of rules. They are more relaxed, laidback and easy going.

Look the way a person constructs their cursive "y" to gather more about his or her personality. The length and breadth of "y" can be very revealing. A skinnier or thinner "y" may indicate a person who is choosy about his or her friends, while a thicker "y" represents them being more open about associating with different types of people. These people love to surround themselves with lots of friends and social acquaintances.

Similarly, a long "y" indicates a love for travel, explorations, and adventures, while a shorter cursive "y" may reflect a need to seek the familiar comfort of their home, and people they are comfortable with.

A more rounded "s" indicates a person's need to keep their loved ones happy and cheerful. They seldom engage in arguments or confrontations, and generally, maintain a positive atmosphere wherever they go. A more pointed "s" reveals a personality that is laborious, ambitious and inquisitive about ideas. Notice how the cursive "s" sometimes widens at the lower end.

This is a sign that the writer may be dissatisfied with their current job, relationship or life. They may not be pursuing what their heart genuinely desires.

Page Margins

Do people leave spaces near the edges or do they write all around the margin? Someone who leaves a huge gap on the page's left side may live in the past. Similarly, a person who leaves a large space on the right-hand side of the margin may be anxious about the future. People who write everywhere on the page possess a mind racing with thoughts and ideas.

Signature

Professional graphologists can tell a lot about a person simply by looking at his or her signature. An illegible or incomprehensible signature is a sign of a person who doesn't like to reveal too much about himself or herself. They closely guard their privacy and may tend to be reserved. On the other hand, a prominent, legible signature is a sign of a person who is confident, self-assured, open and content.

Notice how some people only scrawl in the name of signature? It can indicate that the person is always in a hurry, impatient and wants to do several things at a time. Similarly, a carefully crafted and neat signature is a sign of a person who is independent, meticulous, organized and precise.

Signatures that end with an upward stroke reveal a personality that is confident, ambitious and loves challenges. They aren't afraid to dream and chase seemingly impossible dreams. Likewise, signatures that end with a downward stroke indicate a personality that is low on ambition, self-esteem, and self-confidence. These people are more likely to be overwhelmed by challenges and may not be very goal driven.

Slanting Letters

Some people write with a clear left or right side slant, while others keep their letters flawlessly straight. When a person bends towards the right-hand side, they may be easy going, congenial, open to new experiences and eager to associate with new people.

Similarly, people whose letters tend to slant towards the left-hand side are most likely introverts who enjoy their solidarity. They prefer to remain anonymous while letting others grab the limelight. An upright handwriting reflects the logical, level-headed, and even-tempered person who is ambivalent by nature.

Now, there is small pointer here to avoid misreading people. The above-mentioned analysis is exactly the opposite if you are analyzing a left-handed person. If a left-handed individual slants their letters to the right, they tend to be shy and reserved introverts. Similarly, if they slant their letters to the left, they may be more outgoing extroverts.

Writing Pressure

The intensity of pressure with which a person writes can also reveal a lot about his or her personality. If the handwriting is too dark or written with intense pressure (you'll spot indentation on the back or next page), the person may be volatile, aggressive and stubborn. He or she may not be too accepting of ideas or beliefs that do not match his or her own ideas.

On the other hand, people who write with little pressure or intensity may be more empathetic and sensitive to the needs of others. They may also be more compassionate but may lack energy, enthusiasm, passion, intensity, and liveliness.

Writing That Stands Out

Look out for writing that stands out from the rest of the document. For instance, if the text is otherwise written in a more spaced out and large writing, with only some parts rammed together, it can be a sign of uncertainty or dishonesty.

Summing It Up

While studying someone's handwriting can offer a reasonably accurate insight about an individual's personality, it isn't 100% foolproof (much like every other people analyzing technique). It has its own limitations and flaws. Sometimes people tend to write in a hurry, which can change their writing. Similarly, the way people write a job application letter may differ from the way they write a love letter.

If you want an accurate analysis of an individual's personality, look at different personality reading methods such as reading their body language or verbal communication patterns. Combining different technique will offer you a more comprehensive, in-depth and accurate insight of the person's fundamental personality.

Chapter Four:
Tips For Unlocking Insights about Other People's Values

Mind reading is no magic. It is a science and skill that is painstakingly mastered by a majority of successful people in the world. Being able to read people is a gift that comes handy just about anywhere from approaching your boss for a raise to understanding your client's needs to asking someone out for a date.

Here are some tips for decoding people's values and desires through their cognitive thoughts and actions.

8. Begin With Generational Differences

Though this may not come across as a very accurate technique for decoding a person's values, it can act as a good baseline for understanding the glasses through which a particular person perceives life. Generational differences can be more intriguing than we believe.

While millennials may often believe in impersonal, non-face-to-face communication and believe in articulating their thoughts through blogs or social media, boomers may prefer person, face to face interactions. Identifying the generation a person belongs to can be helpful while approaching an individual or establishing a relationship with him or her.

For instance, if you are looking to seal a deal with a millennial CEO, you'll know that there are fewer chances of him or her wanting to finish all the formalities in person. They are someone who moves with time and will be comfortable sending documents back and forth via email. A virtual presentation may work just fine for them. However, if the CEO is a baby boomer, he or she will prefer the old-fashioned 'spending money and taking potential associates for lunch or dinner' route. Identifying an individual's generation can offer several insights into his or her values.

9. Watch People's Hot Buttons

What are the emotional triggers for a person you want to study? What does their comfort zone comprise of? Knowing people's emotional triggers can offer a good insight into their value system and desires.

My favorite tip is to learn more about people's values by asking open-ended questions. Rather than sticking to yes/no questions, try and ask questions that will elicit in-depth answers, which act as a window for the person's values.

10. Power

The manner in which people handle power or treat people who aren't as powerful as them, reveals a lot about their values or character. What is a person's attitude towards people who he or she perceives to be 'beneath' them? How does the person treat waiters at a restaurant or a customer service advisor? What is their attitude towards children and animals?

The way a person treats someone who can do absolutely nothing in return for him or her speaks volumes about his or her values. Are they particularly rude to people below their level of power? Do they engage in selfless acts? All these reveal a person's true color.

11. Reaction to Criticism

The manner in which a person reacts to criticism reveals a lot about his or her values. How does a person react to being criticized? Do they get into a fit of rage and lash out at the person criticizing them or do they coolly accept the criticism and work hard to improve on their weaknesses? Someone who handles criticism gracefully is more self-assured, confident and frank. They are not egoistic and desire to actively work on their flaws.

Similarly, people who snap on being criticized may suffer from issues related to self-confidence and self-esteem. They may need constant reinforcement of the fact that they are the best and nothing they ever do can be wrong (ego massage). These folks may suffer from a false sense of self-importance or self-entitlement. They also tend to be more egoistic. You may have to handle their fragile ego tactfully.

12. Look At The Person's Social Circle

This is no secret and has been around from the days of "man is known by the company he keeps." One of the best ways for gaining insights into a person's values and desires is through his social circle. Is he or she with the same set of friends since several years? Are they influencers within their social circle or do they lurk in the background? What are the types of people they dislike and avoid?

When I want to know more about a person's values, I always ask them the type of people they keep away from. It gives me a fairly good idea about the ideologies which clash with their own. For instance, when people tell me they don't like to associate with people who are too frivolous or partying all the time, I know these are the guys who are hard-working and goal-oriented. They are ambitious and want to accomplish something in life.

There will be something common in all the people they dislike. This trait will reveal their values. For instance, I noticed that one of my co-workers vehemently despised some people working with us. On closer observation and understanding of their personalities, I realized that all of them had one thing in common. They were all poor listeners who did not care about other people's feelings, thoughts, and opinions. All they did was focus on being heard without attempting to listen to people. This made me realize that the co-worker who hated them had a more empathetic personality and values and placed a high premium on listening to and understanding other people's feelings.

13. Language

A person's values, character, and desires are revealed to a large extent by his or choice of words. According to psychology experts, we tend to focus more on the adjectives we use than pronouns, which makes them subconscious indicators of an individual's personality. When people don't pay too much attention to their pronoun usage, they unveil a lot through it. A large number of personal pronouns indicate an egocentric or self-centered personality. It can also represent high honesty and integrity. It can also be a sign of high self-awareness or someone who is totally clued into their strengths and weaknesses.

There are many other factors such as if a person tries to use big or fancy words to make his or her point, they have a deep desire to impress others or be accepted. The person may have faced rejection or lack of attention during their childhood, which has caused them to develop feelings of low self-esteem. Similarly, people using simple words may be to the point, rational individuals who don't seek attention and are more self-assured or confident.

People who tend to use words such "except," "without" "but" etc. may most likely be honest and genuine as truthful individuals don't hesitate to offer details.

People who are happy and content don't tend to use "I" very often. Also, individuals who use the word "she," "he" "them" and "they" tend to be more focused on other people and relationships.

Even the type of jokes a person narrates or shares can reveal a lot about his or her values, attitude or character.

14. Manner in Which Someone Spends Their Money and Time

How a person spends his or her time and money is a huge indicator of their values, attitude towards life and personality. Time and money are precious commodities for people and how people spend these valuable resources can offer useful insights into their character.

Do they spend a lot of time and money on recreation activities? Do they invest time and money in building a future for themselves and their loved ones? Do they focus on learning, education, and classes? What are their hobbies and passions? Of course, I am not suggesting you go snooping around what people do with their money. All I am saying is observe how people use their finances to know their values and ideals.

15. Their Reaction to No

How do people react when someone says no to them? Are they gracious and respectful and enough to accept it? Do they react in a more volatile and violent manner? Do they respect boundaries set by others? Does the individual then go on to manipulate the decision to get a "yes" from the other person? A person's reaction to "no" can reveal volumes about how he or she is as a person.

16. Gut Feeling

You can learn all the scientific people reading techniques in the world and still rely on your instinct when it comes to reading and analyzing people. If you have a particularly bad feeling about something or someone persistently and can't pin it down to a rational thought or occurrence, it may most likely be instinct or intuition.

Though it doesn't seem like it, even our gut feeling is a deeply scientific process that is closely linked to the limbic brain. It is merely responding to subconscious clues that our conscious mind hasn't caught yet. If you get a feeling that a person is not right for you, your gut feeling may be right!

Chapter Five:
Rebranding Yourself Using Body Language

While meeting people for the first time, we're all eager to make a killer first impression. There is an undisputed eagerness to say and do all the right things at the right time. Much as you'd like to believe that everything you say is making an impression on you, what you are leaving unsaid also says a lot about you.

Nonverbal communication (including body language, gestures, and tone of one's voice) plays an equally important role when it comes to rebranding yourself or wowing people. You can say everything you want to verbally but still not leave the desired impression because your body language is not making a wow impression or isn't compatible with what you are verbally expressing.

Even people who aren't trained to read people through body language can subconsciously latch on to signals that your nonverbal communication or body language gives.

Here are some tips for creating the perfect impression with body language.

17. Keep a Relaxed Posture

Stand straight in a relaxed and easy position but don't lighten up so much that you look too casual or nervous. The worst you can do is sport a slouching posture. Make sure to be mindful, purposeful and conscious of your posture now and then. A hunched back is a sign of being nonchalant or nervous/unsure about a situation. When you keep your posture upright in a more relaxed manner, you not just look confident but also feel more confident subconsciously.

Firm Handshake

A firm handshake is a sign of self-assuredness, confidence and high self-esteem. With a firm grip, you give the impression that you are totally in control of yourself and everything around you. You'll get added points for making direct eye contact and smiling while shaking hands with a person for the first time. It shows you are genuinely pleased to meet the person and are interested in what they have to say.

Be careful of keeping the handshake firm and not crushing his or her hand or you'll come across as increasingly aggressive, and he or she may subconsciously dislike you immediately. You want to come across as confident and in control not overbearing.

A weak, limp and listless handshake, on the other hand, can signify an uncertain, nervous and inhibited personality. It reveals a timid persona and lack of self-confidence.

Mirroring the Person's Actions

Man is wired since primitive times to show affiliation towards another human through mirroring his or her actions. It is so deeply embedded in the subconscious mind that we don't even realize it is happening.

Now that you know it, use this information to your advantage. When you mirror people's actions, they form a subconscious connection with you, and view you as "one of their kind." The result, they end up forming a favorable impression of you or liking you almost immediately.

The act of mirroring should be gradual and discreet, not very obvious or the person will think you are mimicking them, which will be counterproductive. If the person is leaning against the bar while speaking to you, you do the same slowly. If they raise their glass to take a sip of the drink, follow suit. If they move their weight from one leg to another, gradually attain the same posture.

Look at the way they are using their hands. What are the gestures they make frequently? What are the typical words and phrases used by them? Try to mirror their gestures, expressions, and words. Match the tone of the voice. What is the typical manner in which they speak? Do they speak in a restrained, hush –hush tone? Or are they loud and enthusiastic while speaking? Observe all this and try to incorporate as much of their verbal and nonverbal patterns as possible without making it too obvious.

Body language experts suggest aligning your body with the body of the person you are communicating with. Position your body to face him or her directly. This reveals your interest in engaging with him or her or giving them your complete attention, which everyone appreciates.

If the person you want to make a favorable impression on is standing in a group, and it isn't possible to directly face him or her, don't try to cut people off or leave them out of the conversation.

Rather, pivot your attention strategically towards the person you want to impress by making frequent eye contact with him or her (even while addressing the group), and offering a friendly smile. Don't stop a conversation and move your body towards him or her when in a group. It will only make you look eager to impress and overbearing.

Keep Legs and Arms Uncrossed

This may not be important when you are communicating casually with a close friend or family members. However, it holds plenty of importance when you are communicating with someone for the first time and want to create a stellar first impression. Like we discussed earlier, it is a defensive position. People will view you as guarded, closed and secretive. You are less likely to come across as a genuine, open and honest person. Crossing arms and legs can also be a signal of disinterest (pray don't do it on a first date or that all important client negotiation) or absolute boredom.

Proxemics

Use proxemics to your advantage by maintaining appropriate physical space between you and the person you want to impress. Proxemics is nothing but the study of physical space when it comes to nonverbal communication.

Psychologists and body language experts believe that the amount of physical space a person leaves while interacting with another person reveals a lot about the dynamics of their relationship or the equation between the two. When you are meeting a person for the first time and trying to make a favorable impression, do not try to invade their personal space.

Maintain a minimum distance of four feet between with him or her as a rule of the thumb until you get to know them better. You can demonstrate your interest by leaning slightly in the direction of the person but don't attempt to get too physically close to them too soon. Even if you aren't leaning ahead, ensure that you don't lean behind. Just maintain a steady, relaxed and upright posture. Leaning back can signify lack of interest or boredom.

Small Talk Does Big Magic

Verbal exchange plays a huge role in determining the impression you create on a person. Learn something about the person before you meet them or attempt to strike a conversation with them. Digging a little into their background on the social media will give you a good idea about their likes, dislikes, hobbies, professional, etc.

Does he or she volunteer at a community organization? Do they play golf? What are the things you have in common with this person? These are good starting points for making a meaningful and engaging conversation.

One of my favorite tips for making a favorable first impression on people through small talk is going through the entire newspaper or browsing the net for the day's most happening news stories. If nothing else works, you can start by making a conversation about world events. This will make you come across as an engaging and well-informed conversationalist.

Just ensure that you don't share your views or opinion on something controversial, religious or political and you'll do fine. Stick to general, non-controversial topics such as new discoveries, path-breaking research, advancement in technology, weather, global economy, etc. Small talk indeed goes a long mile when it comes to making a favorable first impression.

Show Attentiveness and Courtesy

I'll let you in on a secret. One of the best ways to be instantly likable and desirable to people is to listen to them. And listening doesn't mean having your ear in their direction. It means giving them your undivided attention and acknowledging what they are saying.

You can offer plenty of verbal and nonverbal clues that you are keenly listening to the person in the form of nodding your head, verbally acknowledging what he or she is saying and paraphrasing their sentences to show you are closely listening to what they are saying.

Chapter Five: Rebranding Yourself Using Body Language

Do not, I repeat, do not keep looking at your phone or pretend to be distracted. If you want to make a favorable impression on the person, give him or her undivided attention, demonstrate good manners and be polite/courteous towards everyone around. Mirror the other person's actions naturally.

Chapter Six:
Reading People through Their Words

The eyes may very well be the windows to a person's mind and soul, but their words reveal how they think, process information or offer insights into their character. Words represent both thoughts and feelings. Listening to a person's words can reveal a lot about his or her inner thoughts and ideas. Specific words can indicate the behavioral traits of a person who said or wrote them. These are words clues that help you predict the person's characteristics almost accurately. Though you may not be able to read their entire personality through words, you get a good idea about the behavioral patterns and thought the process of a person.

Our brain is nothing short of a marvel. While thinking, we tend to use more of nouns and verbs. On the other hand, when we try to express these thoughts in spoken or written form, we emphasize on adjectives and adverbs.

The basic structure of a sentence comprises a verb and subject such as "I ate." Any more words that are added to the subject (I) and verb (ate) can offer clues into the individual's behavioral characteristics. Any words added to a basic sentence help you make educated guesses about the person. For example, if a person says he or she walked briskly, it can indicate a sense of urgency. They may walk briskly or quickly, owing to their need to be on time for an appointment, which demonstrates a more conscientious mindset.

People may also walk quickly out of fear or when there is a threat. It can be a threat in a potentially dangerous neighborhood or bad weather. When someone uses the word quickly, watch out for more clues about why he or she has chosen to use that particular word. Here are some pointers to read people through their word clues.

18. I worked really hard to accomplish my dreams

The word hard here suggests that the person loves to chase goals that are challenging to accomplish and doesn't like anything that comes

easy. It can also be an indication that the
particular goal he or she is referring to was
particularly tough compared to the ones he or
she achieved earlier. Using words such as "hard"
also reflect a mindset that is ready to postpone
gratification to accomplish his or her long-term
goals. He or she most likely holds the view that
dedication, perseverance and hard work is the
key to producing stellar results.

At times, people convey a lot through what they
leave unsaid.

Let us try understanding this with an example.

You are a server at one of the plushiest fine
dining restaurants in your city. It serves multi-
course meals that are much sought after by
patrons. You have a family over at the restaurant
for a multi-course meal one evening, and warmly
welcome them. As a server, you introduce them
to each course and offer interesting trivia behind
each of the preparations, keeping them
enthralled. You are sure they've had a wonderful
time and enjoyed their meal. When they've paid
the check and are about to walk out, you ask
them if they liked the food. The man says, "The
soup was good!" You aren't pleased. Why? Did

he say the soup was good right? What do you think is the reason for your disappointment?

The answer lies in focusing on what he left unsaid. When the man said the soup was nice, he indirectly implied that the rest of the food or other courses weren't as good as the soup or were average. They were nothing to talk about. This is precisely the reason why we sometimes get offended when someone looks surprised and says, "you are looking good today." What they leave unsaid is, you don't normally look this good every day. Thus, while people convey a lot through the words they use, they also communicate a lot through the words they leave unsaid.

I made up my mind to buy that home

If a person says he or she has decided to do something or made up his or her mind to something often, they may have considered many options before arriving at a decision. It means the person may be more contemplative and take his or her time to weight his or her options before concluding. They deliberate upon their decisions and are more analytical by nature. There are very slim chances of him or her being a rash or impulsive decision maker. These are more signs of an introvert than extrovert personality.

However don't be quick to jump to conclusions as soon as someone uses the word "decided." Look for a pattern and other clues that point to a more reflective, thinking and introvert personality. A definitive personality assessment needs thorough psychological observation and assessment, and making sweeping conclusions about people based on a few words will only land you in trouble.

Extroverts gather their energies from others and seek greater environmental stimulation. They tend to use the trial and error method rather than deliberating upon a decision. Introverts will rarely speak without thinking, while extroverts tend to be more spontaneous.

It helps if you know beforehand whether a person is an introvert or extrovert to mold your communication pattern according to their predominant personality. For instance, if you are a salesperson, knowing whether your prospective client is an introvert or extrovert will help you determine how he or she makes decisions.

Introverts take time to mull over things and make up their mind. Similarly, if you are negotiating an important business deal, it is important to understand if the other person displays characteristic of an introvert or extrovert.

If you notice a predominantly introverted mindset, give them more time to think before they take a decision. Pushing them into making a quick decision may go against you (they will most likely respond in the negative if they aren't given enough time to consider their decision).

On the other hand, a person who shows signs of making quick decisions may be an extrovert. These people can be goaded into taking fast decisions and actions. They can be pressurized into making instant decisions because they are more comfortable doing things without thinking excessively about them. However, one of the most important considerations is that people rarely exhibit a completely introvert or extrovert personality. Most people are a combination of both. They like to be around other people but also value personal time and space.

Uses of words such as "right" and "wrong" often

Notice how people often say things such as "I did the right or wrong thing." These words suggest a strong inclination towards ethics and morals. It reveals that they may have overcome an ethical dilemma that helped them make a just or unjust decision, which has either made them happy or disillusioned. Using the word "right" all the time demonstrates a strong character and the need to be ethical. They most likely make the right judgment even when there is a conflict or when they are confronted with an opposing view.

When you tune in carefully to people's words and listen to what he or she is saying, their words can reveal a lot.

I sat patiently through his or her talks

Like we discussed earlier, the adverbs a person uses in a basic sentence helps describe his or her state of mind, thoughts or feelings. For instance, if the person is said to have patiently listened to someone, it means he or she wasn't making much sense or that they were boring. Perhaps the person had to attend to nature's call and still sat patiently through someone's talk.

Irrespective of the reason of why he or she said that it implies that they were preoccupied with another thing. This is an individual who listens to social etiquettes and customs, while not offending established norms.

If you are interviewing someone for job recruitment purposes, this may most likely be your ideal candidate who respects authority, establishments and rules.

Talking about others

Haven't we all heard that all famous quote about how what we say about us reveals plenty about us?

In a study conducted by Peter Harms at the University of Nebraska, and Siminie Vazire at the Washington University in St. Louis (published in the Journal of Personality and Social Psychology) it was found that simply by asking a group of participants to rate negative and positive characteristics of three people helped researchers understand the each participant's mental health, overall well-being, social attitude and the way they were perceived by others.

Chapter Six: Reading People through Their Words

It was found that a person's tendency to see others in a more positive light was a reflection of his or her own positive personality traits. He or she viewed others pretty much with the same filters that he or she used for themselves. There was a strong co-relation between judging others in a positive light and being happy, enthusiastic, courteous, compassionate, emotionally stable and able themselves. Talking about other people is positive, encouraging words is a huge sign of how overall satisfied people are with their lives, and how they are viewed by other people around them.

Conversely, negative words used to describe others are highly linked with antisocial behavior, overall dissatisfaction with their life, narcissism, and a low sense of self-worth. People with predominantly negative traits tend to view and speak to others in a negative or unflattering manner. It can also be an indicator of personality disorders or mental health issues.

Chapter Seven:
Reading People through Their Environment

Aperson's immediate environment can reveal a lot about his or her, and I don't mean the pop psychology quizzes that keep pooping on your timeline. I mean it is a solid, scientific way to make educated guesses about a person's character. There are psychological principles behind analyzing a person's behavior through his or her immediate environment.

Here are a bunch of awesome, proven tips for reading a person through his or her surroundings.

19. Colors

The first thing you notice when you enter someone's home is the colors used in the décor. A person's choice of colors can psychologically reveal several aspects of their personality. For instance, if the person is using a lot of bright, bold colors such as red, orange, electric blue, etc., he or she is unafraid to take risks or articulating their thoughts. Their personality is bolder, outgoing and adventure bitten. They are not afraid to say things as they see it.

Subtle colors may imply that the person is more subtle, restrained and reflective in nature. They may be deep thinkers who weigh all options carefully before taking an important decision.

People who are more focused inwards or introverts tend to do up their homes on solid, soft hues and more muted patterns, while outgoing personalities tend to use bold, experimental designs.

The Hidden Closet

The mess in your house probably reveals the mess in your head too! No, that's not being judgmental. It is a way to analyze how people's thoughts and mind leads to the creation of their environment. A neat, organized, efficiently categorized work desk is a sign of a mind that possess great clarity of thought. Excessive cleanliness or orderliness can also be a sign of anxiety, nervousness or low self-esteem. It can also point to a mental health issue such as obsessive-compulsive disorder. Watch out for signs of extreme orderliness and an obsession with cleanliness.

On the contrary, people whose spaces are more chaotic and disorganized looking can reveal a cluttered and disorganized mind. It can be a sign of being good at many things or multitasking. When you are engaged in too many activities, you barely have the time to organize your space, which means it is often left unattended or in a disorganized manner. Sometimes, it can be a sign of plain laziness or lack of clarity/objectives in life.

It has been observed that people with a more extrovert personality tend to have more chaos around them. Their drawers will most likely be messy and disorganized. On the contrary, people who are more reflective and introvert by nature will spend more time meticulously organizing, arranging and prioritizing their belongings.

A majority of people (however picky about cleanliness) have some areas of the home that are a hidden mess. Think under the bed or behind their closets. These are mostly areas that are not often accessed by people and therefore neglected. If a person keeps even these inaccessible areas neat and organized, they may be suffering from anxiety. These are the most likely the type of people who are control freaks or are obsessed with being completely in control of everything around them.

Studies also reveal that a messy, disorganized and erratic environment is a sign of high creativity. People living in such places tend to generate better and more path-breaking ideas. So yes, the cliché about an artist of scientist/inventor with messy hair and a disorganized look is actually true from the psychological perspective.

Prints

Amusing as it sounds, I can tell a lot about a person simply by looking at the prints they use in their décor or on their clothes. Big, bright and bold prints reveal that the person is more self-assured, confident and not inhibited by other's opinion of him or her. They are most likely fiercely independent in thought and action, and original thinkers. They have their own clear opinion/views on several issues and aren't easily influenced by others.

Similarly, quirky prints such as polka dots or animals or comic legends can reveal a fun, whimsical, creative and original personality. Geometric prints, on the other hand, reveal a need for order and organization.

A study conducted by researchers at Yale concluded that people who spend a long time on showers and bathing are mostly lonely. They use the warmth of the bath as a substitute for the lack of emotional warmth.

Psychologists have also deciphered the meaning of having a wall filled with motivational quotes, messages, and posters. According to experts, this is most likely an indicator of neuroticism. These folks use their immediate environment to soothe their nerves and help them sail through. Don't immediately conclude something is wrong with a person or that he/she needs help if they have a wall full of motivational posters. Talk to them more to gain a better understanding of their personality or observe them closely to gather non-verbal clues.

Old Items

People whose spaces are filled with items from the past such as old job uniforms, sports team jerseys that no longer fit, clothes that they've outgrown, etc. are the ones who most likely live in the past or are unable to let go of their past. They cling to memories and often refuse to move on. Hoarding things belonging to their past is not a sign that they are attached to the belongings per se. These people are in fact clinging to the memories associated with these belongings.

Chapter Eight:
Determining Personality through Birth Order

Analyzing people through their birth order isn't just a bunch of stereotypes or cocktail party talk but a fairly accurate manner of predicting someone's personality based on their childhood experiences. Our birth order often determines the roles we play in our families or the status quo we are given during our early childhood years, which ultimately shapes our fundamental personality or the way we relate to others.

Even though it seems like a study in pop psychology, subconsciously the way we relate to our immediate family members during early childhood has a deep impact on the way we turn out as adults. Many parents will vehemently confirm the fact that each of the children is different from the other regarding personality, though they are all raised in the same house/environment.

There are several factors that along with birth order determine the personality of an individual, and these factors are so closely woven that they cannot be isolated while studying an individual's personality of his or her birth order. Some of these factors are: number of family members or children in the family, the family's socioeconomic status, the parent's education level, environmental factors, and more.

Alfred Adler (an associate of Sigmund Freud and Carl Jung) was the first to propose the theory of determining an individual's personality through his or her birth order while analyzing his clients. However, it was psychologist Frank Sulloway of MIT who modernized the theory for contemporary application.

In his path-breaking book, Born to Rebel Sulloway named five primary traits that defined a person, which are extraversion, neuroticism, openness, agreeableness, and consciousness. According to him, a person's birth order impacted all these fundamental traits. He made a startling conclusion that people who have the same birth order have more in common personality-wise than siblings who are raised together. This is because, according to him, a person's birth-rank impacts them more than his or her environment.

According to author and parenting expert Grose, two children never assume the same role within a family. We all automatically and instinctively take on roles within groups without realizing it. Our families are often the first group we are exposed to. The dynamics that define the role we take on in the very first group largely influence our personality.

Here are a few tips for reading people through their birth order.

20. First Born

The stereotype of firstborn individuals is that they are natural leaders, ambitious by nature and innately responsible. This is partly true because for some time the child doesn't have any competition when it comes to earning the affection and attention of family members. They don't have to compete with siblings for time and attention from parents. This gives them a slight edge over siblings.

Again, they tend to be caretakers or surrogate parents for their younger siblings (often teaching them things the older child has learned before, the younger siblings). This makes them develop leadership skills and a more accountable, responsible nature. They are protective by nature, and often lead the way for others.

On the flipside, if parents place great expectations on the firstborn, and he or she feels incapable of matching up to those expectations, they can develop a damaging personality that is marked by low self-esteem, the constant need for validation and acceptance from others, low self-confidence and a general feeling of never being good enough for anything or anyone.

According to Sulloway's research, firstborn showed more signs of conformism for rules and respect for authority/tradition. They demonstrate signs of respecting the established status quo rather than challenging it.

A study about firstborns reveals that they tend to be more goal-oriented and place high importance on success and accomplishments. Their place in the birth order makes them lean towards achievements. The first born's personality may also be marked by a constant need to be control and authority, at times making them appear bossy or dogmatic. They are almost always concerned about other's approval.

As per Sulloway's birth order theory, firstborns who are considerably physically stronger than their younger siblings are likely to demonstrate dominant behavioral traits.

Some typical traits of first-born people are – goal oriented, responsible, determined, conformists and meticulous/detail oriented.

Middle Borns

Middle borns often have a more complex personality because they don't enjoy the special rights of the oldest child nor the leeway or privileges of the youngest child. They are awkwardly juxtaposed between the two, owing to which they turn out to be excellent negotiators or peacemakers. These are also people who have a wider social circle as they rely on friends for attention and support when parents focus more on the youngest or oldest sibling.

In case the oldest child doesn't fit the role of a leader at home, the middle child takes his or her place or fills their shoes. Also, there can, in fact, be several middle children. How does one determine their personality in such a scenario? For example, in a family of five children, there can be three middle children. As a rule of the thumb, each child shows personality traits that are different from the one immediately next to him or her in order. This means that within the three middle children, the first and last will have more similar traits than the middle one.

Middleborns are typically social by nature and are obsessed by a sense of fairness and peace. They are known for their excellent negotiation skills, which make them good diplomats and peacemakers.

While the oldest child enjoys undivided attention from parents, while the youngest can get away with murder, family's middle baby is often left with neither. Since they are literally juxtaposed in the middle, they turn out to be amazing compromisers, peacemakers, and negotiators. These kids are harder to pin down and are more loyal, faithful and relationship-oriented by nature. They seldom let down people who trust them or are close to them.

Middle borns typically display these personality traits – they are peacemakers, flexible, accommodating, diplomatic, free-spirited and magnanimous. They are known to work well in teams and relate well with people who are younger or older to them in age or authority since they have a more amiable nature. Middleborns are also known to be competent in more than a single skill.

Last Born

The last born is often known to be a charmer and risk taker. They are more free-spirited, creative and adventurous. There is a tendency to reinvent the wheel rather than following established rules and norms.

Parents tend to be less careful and cautious with the last born since they've already lived through the experience of being a parent at least once and aren't as overwhelmed by the prospect as when they became parents for the first time. Also, parents generally tend to be more financially well off than they were during the birth of the first child, which means there is a tendency to indulge the child more.

Parents are more relaxed when it comes to following rules, which means the youngest child doesn't develop traits of a conformist. They are used to being pampered and showered by attention. Since parents are more lenient with youngest borns, they don't tend to be very rule oriented or revere established authority. There is a tendency to make their own rules, and create new paths rather than walking commonly walked paths.

Typical personality traits revealed by last borns are rebelliousness, empathy, creativity, high sense of self-worth or self-esteem and stubborn. The youngest child often displays traits related to attention-seeking, sociability, extroversion, and manipulativeness. They make for great sales professionals and know how to get their way around people.

A study conducted in 2001 revealed that last-born children show an inclination for careers related to creative arts, and the outdoors. On the contrary, firstborns show an inclination for intellectual vocations.

Only Child

Now, again, the stereotype about an only child being self-centered or creative is not entirely without a strong reason. Since they spend a lot of time in solitary activities, they tend to be creative, entertaining and innovative. They always find resourceful ways to keep themselves busy, earning self-entertainment skills.

Much like first-borns who get used to having their parents' undivided attention until their siblings are born, only children are often self-assured, confident, meticulous and articulate. Since only children don't have to compete with siblings for their parents' attention or material belongings, they tend to develop a sense of self-entitlement and self-centeredness.

They get used to having things their way and find it challenging to cope when things do not happen as they desire. Firstborns always want to be the important people around and have a hard time sharing the limelight with others. Another most marked trait about only child is they are perfectionists. Owing to the fact that their only role models are their parents or other adults in the family, they tend to become huge perfectionists.

21. Factors That Make the Reading More Accurate

There are many factors influencing an individual's personality that can make your reading more accurate. Psychologists often suggest looking at a person's siblings while analyzing his or her personality since two children within the family rarely share the same role. You will know the role played by the individual you wish to analyze by observing his or her siblings.

Some other factors affecting your reading are genetics and gender. A majority of our personality is determined by gender and genetics in addition to the birth order, which means these are also factors worth considering while analyzing a person's birth order.

Conclusion

Thank you for downloading the book, How To Analyze People: *21 Fundamental Techniques to Interpret Body Language, Personality Types, Human Psychology and Secretly Analyze People.*

I sincerely hope it has offered you several valuable insights into reading people's personality through proven strategies, tried and tested subconscious techniques and a treasure trove of practical tips. These tips can be applied just anywhere, in any situation from business to interpersonal relationships to social settings to negotiations.

Whether you want to figure out the personality of a potentially big client during a negotiation or the characteristics of the hot new prospective date you have your eyes on, this book is a handy resource for helping you read others effectively. If there's a single largest skill that spells success in today's world, it is the ability to read people.

This allows you to mold your message according to the personality of the other person to accomplish optimally beneficial communication.

The next step is to use the book and apply it in your daily life in small, gradual ways to begin with. Start by observing people at the airport or doctor's clinic when you have some time at hand. The interest will quickly catch on, and you'll find yourself taking a deep interest in reading and analyzing people.

Lastly, if you enjoyed reading the book, please take the time to share your views by posting a review on Amazon. It'd be greatly appreciated!

Printed in Great Britain
by Amazon